Can You Please Me?

De'Vina Jackson

TABLE OF CONTENTS

De'Vina Jackson

Preface

First, let me start by thanking you all for supporting my form of therapy. I have been writing poetry for over twenty years and it wasn't until about five years ago that I started sharing my poems. Every time I've put pen to paper it has been because I've been inspired to write. A memory, a relationship, a movie, book or a conversation; each moment has shaped a poem of mine in its own individual way. These poems are a collection of the emotions or thoughts I was feeling based on that particular moment in time. We have all had moments that either emotionally drain or uplift us. This is a collection of some of the poems that have helped me through some of those moments.

Poetry for me has always been therapeutic. It has always given me some relief against the current stresses in my life. As I share with you the memories of my joys, pains, tears, love and arousal. I can only hope that you can connect with my words in order to find your own therapy through me.

De'Vina Jackson

Can you please me?

I need a man who listens to what I have to say.
I need a man who wants it when I do,
And wants it when I don't.
A man that's not lazy.
A man pumping harder than I'm pumping.
A man willing to try new things.
Oh yeah, that's this poet's dream.
I need a man who waits up for me.
Who rubs my feet.
I need a man to love me, without suffocating me.
A man who can hold me, without holding me captive.
A man who is going to embrace me, without
imprisoning me.
He understands my need to succeed.
Is that the kind of man you can be?
I want a man to kiss my body from head to toe.
Sucking my finger and slurping my toes.
I need emotions so intense, as I enjoy my erotic
consciousness.
I need a man that gives a thousand kisses.
Each kiss an apology for the multiple orgasms he
plans to give.
I need a man who abuses me with passion.
I need seduction, not just sex.
Can you be the man for me?

1

Can You Please Me?

Will you be my erotic and exotic fisher man?
Can you use your tongue to fish for treats?
To find my pearl?
Will you play with my piercings?
Are you a man who loves to eat?
I need a man who wants to explore.
He should explore me and all of my deadly sins.
Punish me for my good deeds.
Make me want to swallow your seed.
Do you sound like the kind of man I need?
I need penetration.
Deep and slow so intoxicating.
I need a man to drip oil down my back.
Slip his hands into my crack.
Tantalize my chocolate star.
As
Lips and tongue sip on my sweetest nectars.
I need a man that's not afraid of six legs and two clits
in one bed.
I need a man that likes to hit it from the back.
He understands that some women like it like that.
It's not a power position or a nice view of my ass.
Its how you can go deeper and when I throw it back
on you.
You are not the least bit surprised.
You're not scared.
And you're not gonna run from it because you can't
handle it.
I want a man who likes to spank and be spanked.
He knows the sound of skin hitting skin makes me
wet just thinking about it.
A man that likes to get head while he is driving.
A man that knows that while I'm sucking his dick I'm
getting hot and wet.
He understands I suck because I enjoy it.

2

Can You Please Me?

The type of man that will pull over and fuck me on the
hood of his car.
Will you be the man to help me become a porno
star?
The man that I need has a homicidal dick.
The type of dick that makes my yoni feel murdered.
It gives me that uneasy feeling.
You know like,
looking at a murder scene,
but
It's so unbelievable that you can't turn away.
That is a man that can drown me in pleasure.
A multitude of waves rolling over my body.
Do you understand that sometimes I don't want
intercourse?
I don't want to make love.
Sometimes I just want to fuck.
Can you play an instrument?
I want a man that plays a sensual soundtrack across
my body.
His tune is deep kisses.
The pitch is a caress.
The tone tongue lashes.
All creating a chorus of moans.
Ending the symphony in a lustful catastrophic event
called,
An orgasm.
A man that does not expect to paid with pussy.
He knows I give it to him because I feel he deserves
it.
I want a man who will push his manhood inside of me.
Without a care of who may see.
On the beach.
In the sea.
At the park.
In the middle of a parade.

3

Can You Please Me?

Only a bold man can claim these seas.
I want man to give my body therapy.
I want a professor with a PhD in erotology.
I need a man that understands that somedays
penetration is not what I crave.
Only soft stimulation will make my cream cascade.
I need a man that knows that pleasure is in the quality
of the actions taken.
I have to have a man that understands the power of
the clit.
Its sensitivity.
Its raw energy.
It must be savored sweetly.
Licked lavishly.
Nibbled on nicely.
Even though it is compared to a dick.
He knows it is not a dick.
It is my enticing mango meat.
Dripping juices so sticky.
And so sweet.
I need a man that's not afraid to shave me.
Especially if he likes it smooth and very neat.
I want a man that knows there aren't many women
like me.
I need a man who is not afraid to share me intimately.
He knows that no one partner can fulfill all needs
sexually.
I crave a man who knows to give is to receive.
Giving me a heavenly abyss.
Is receiving affirmation that you gave me gratification
Actually, I need a male version of me.
Unfortunately, every man that comes close seems to
be crazy.
This powerful embodiment of sexuality I possess.
Seems to be too much for any man I confess.
That's the reason they are all insane.

Can You Please Me?

I may never find a man that understand me.
But for you that seek my treats.
I Ask…
Are you ready for me?

De'Vina Jackson

Choices

Bittersweet moments in time.
Elusive tenderness.
Playing Russian Roulette in your bed.
Gluttonous with my time.
Becoming an overshare.
Roughly a diamond.
Not disguised.
You overlooking its natural beauty.
Its perfect flaws.
Its pure uniqueness.
Enhanced values.
Stolen.
By your blind lust.
Stolen.
By your wondering eyes.
Stolen.
Always projecting.
My color not right.
My type unfit.
Beneath it all.
It's typical of you.
To be always looking.
Forever seeking.
That fantasy wife.
That replacement girl.
You.
Forever looking for her.
No, your internal compass works.
So I'll explain why you can't find her.

Choices

Your heart aches.
It aches for me.
You get butterflies.
From thoughts of me.
Your blood flows like rivers.
All down into a sea of me.
I am not an optical illusion.
Successfully I have captured,
Your mind.
Your body.
Your heart.
It all
Speaks so highly
Of me.
And still you don't believe.
Here is my resignation.
I'm done fighting for that promotion.
Good day to you, sir.
I'm signing out.
The daughter.
The sister.
The mother
Your lover.
If you have something to say,
I suggest you say it now.
Plead your case.
Or forever you will be searching,
For someone.
With no such luck.
Will you ever find another me.
With no such luck,
Will you find another Queen.

Faith

When love is not enough,
It's time to let go.
When letting go is too hard,
It's time to let God.
When those cracks get to big,
Sealant won't work.
When shutting down can no longer protect,
It's time to prepare for hurt.
When dreams become a nightmares,
In fairy tales I can't believe.
But.
When I see your face,
It inspires me to believe.
When you kiss my lips,
It soothes my hurt.
When you say 'I love you',
It's the only sealant that works.
When I'm faced with fear,
It's time to trust God.

He tells me that he placed you here,
And that with faith your love is always enough.

De'Vina Jackson

She Speaks

I know what you're thinking.
Here we go,
Someone else with a pen.
She's about to get politically deep.
Let her soul speak.
Thinking her words are oh so unique.
Nope.
Not at all.
None of that is why my pen bleeds.
And no…
My words are not unique.
You're probably going through the same shit as I speak.
Maybe a no good baby daddy.
Or a man who beats.
He won't support your mental needs.
Or he just plan cheats.
So most women know a lot about the words I speak.
Oh please.
Some of y'all need to stop with the "amen's" and the
testifying.
You're probably the groupie in row 6 seat C,
Making it capable for him to cheat.
Stop considering yourself a woman or a queen.
Fucking an attached man makes you a whore, sweetie.
But here and now,
This is your deliverance from evil.
Say it with me.
From this day forward, my cookie will be treated
respectfully.
I will respect my cookie, therefore demanding others to
respect it.

She Speaks

So ladies, let your soul speak.
Be proud of being unique.
You don't have to be politically deep to know your worth.
All you have to do is believe.
Value yourself.
To let your soul speak.

The Rebuild

Pardon my dust.
Excuse me, sir.
I have all these pieces to pick up.
Building a new me isn't all that easy.
No time to play.
No time to seek pleasures of the flesh.
It's time to rebuild.
I'm not just talking about my broken heart.
I'm also speaking of my broken spirit.
My broken mental state.
My broken sense of sight.
My broken body.
My Broken…
Vagina.
Giving all parts of myself to an "undeserving".
This "undeserving" name doesn't matter much,
Just know he wasn't worth my touch.
This "undeserving" age doesn't matter much,
Just know he wasn't worth my kiss.
This "underserving" race doesn't matter much,
Just know he wasn't worth my love.
This "undeserving" severed the relationship between
my heart and my brain.
He tainted the river that connected my soul to my
body.
Lifeless and ignorant, I moved through his idea of
commitment.
Everyone could see I deserved more, except me.

The Rebuild

Everyone could decipher his lies that I refused to
decode.
Drowning in his story.
Unable to battle the currents of his sea.
Death becomes her.
Or so it seems.
Just as I decided to end the fight.
Just as I decided to let go of life.
Just as I decided to relax and give up.
Just as I took what I thought was my last breath.
I began to float.
I began to breath.
I began to see.
I saw the horizon and I was happy to be seen.
I was happy to be me.
I saw arms outstretched to save me.
That "undeserving" was no longer standing in my way.
That "undeserving" was no longer my drug of choice.
As I stand here today enjoying the rehabilitation which
is you.
Please pardon my dust.
Just be my crutch.
Because once I make it through my rebuild,
The possibilities.
Will include unconditional love.

Once Upon a Time

There once was a day when I dreamed dreams of
happily-ever-after.
A romantic fairy tale filled with infinite love.
But real love.
Ponder that thought with me.
What makes love real?
Is it arranged?
Is it deranged?
Is it only between a man and a woman?
Real love isn't superficial.
Real love isn't chocolate candies on holidays.
Real love is one single rose picked on your way
home.
Real love is a simple text saying "I miss your face",
Or
"I miss the way you smell".
Real love can meet and exceed doubt and reason.
Sort of like magic.
Sort of like faith.
Sort of like butterfly kisses and waterfalls.
But…
My waterfalls felt like chemical burns,
My dreams of happily-ever-after became reindeer
games.
Nightmares similar to tales from the crypt.
Stories seeming to star the crypt keeper himself.
Filled with tragic cries and rainbow lies.
Ending with a tainted pot of gold.
My happily-ever-after faded away.

Once Upon a Time

Demons cast spells of false hope.
While I try to replay my fairy tale days,
I'm still failing to find my happily-ever-after.
Currently.
Just.
Trying.
To Live.

A Message to My Lover

Stop the Presses!
What does that say?
Are you?
Can you?
Willing?
Nope, unwilling.
Incapable of unconditional.
If you were,
You'd know you must love me.
That's the true meaning of unconditional love.
You must complete me.
When I'm failing,
You must step up.
When I give up,
You must keep going.
Carry me, unconditional lover.
And when I stop being loving,
You have to love me.
And when I start degrading you,
You must love me.
When I start disrespecting you,
You must love me.
When I allow other people to disrespect you,
You must continue to love me.
Hey, unconditional lover.
Oh, unconditional lover.
Do you hear me talking to you?
You know it's not for every woman.
Don't feel bad if you can't handle it.

A Message to My Lover

You know my boys' girl?
She knows what's up.
She's the truth.
She's been through four baby mamas.
She's still there.
She's the truth.
That's real love.
She's real tough.
So, unconditional lover.
I haven't had any babies on you.
All I ever done was cheat on you.
But you know you always gonna be my boo.
So, unconditional lover.
Stop with all the bull shit.
Don't change to a conditional bitch.
If you do, I just have to call it quits.
I need me an unconditional bitch.
Yo unconditional lover.
Aye boo chill I ain't call you no bitch like that.
I'm just using the word.
Damn, you be trippin'.
Aye.
My love is true.
But if you get fat,
Girl, we through.
But baby.
Boo.
You my ace.
It's true.
Don't Believe the lies.
Those bitches want to be you.
This message right here is only for you.
As long as you stay true.
It's us against the world.
Kinda like Bonnie and Clyde,
'Cept we don't die in the end.

A Message to My Lover

We AK's and AR's blazing.
So, unconditional lover.
Can you handle this role?
You know.
Be my leading lady.
The one right by my side.
My number one.
Huh?
Nah, unconditional lover.
What?
You are Number One.
How many others after number "one" don't matter.
They all know about you,
They know they better respect you too,
I let them know they place.
I mean shit.
Why you tranna trap me and shit?
It's only you, girl.
My Numero Uno.
But look, if you cant be the boo,
I'll just replace you too.
Unconditional lover.
Tell me I've found you.
So we can live happily-ever-after.
Whadda ya say?
Aye, Bitch?
You Cool?

De'Vina Jackson

At Odds

What if the timing was different?
What if the people were different?
What if their past was different?
What if their pains were different?

Then the relationship would be different.

Maybe she would smile more.
Maybe he would laugh more.
Maybe he would include her more.
Maybe she would tell him more.

Then the relationship would be different.

Why doesn't she call him her man?
Why doesn't he call her his girl?
Why doesn't he kiss away her tears?
Why doesn't she tell him when she cries?

Then the relationship would be different.

How come she doesn't speak up?
How come he always gets up?
How come he never stays?
How comes she never goes?

Then the relationship would be different.

Is it possible they're both afraid?

At Odds

Is it possible they're both getting played?
Is it possible they're both in love?
Is it possible they're both afraid to say?

Then the relationship will be different.

It could be that they're on different teams.
It could be that they're on different leads.
It could be that they have different lives.
It could be that they have different backgrounds.

Then the relationship would be different.

So, of course they move as mirrored acts.
Neither revealing details or facts.
No one has much to say.
Just going with the flow day by day.

Both too afraid to make the relationship different.

Because I Asked

I just want to be made love to.
The type of love that makes movies seem
like cartoons.
Make love to my mind.
By first.
Exploring my
Mental universe.
Exploring all things that
Make up me.
Ask questions about my past.
With plans to build a better future.
I just want you to,
Make love to me.
Understanding my unique complexity.
The type of love I want to receive was,
Personally created just for me.
That love would include superior intimacy.
An unlimited amount of passion and,
Love making.
If you are to be my king,
You must understand my animalistic need.
Yes, my king.
I need you to bite me.
Yes, my king.
I need you to devour me.
You must also have the ability to lead.
Be forceful.
But always make me cream.
As your queen,

Because I Asked

I plan to satisfy all of your needs.
Offering my body to you.
To do with as you please.
You... My king.
Should deliver me.
You... My king.
Should save me.
Save me from myself.
Save me from my fears.
Save me from my dreams.
Save me from my nightmares,
By creating new memories.
Closing my eyes.
Imagining you,
Caressing me.
Imagining you,
Kissing me.
Your hands moving across my body.
Slowly drifting.
Slowly moving.
Slowly.
Creating electricity.
Creating heat.
My body heat rises.
Rising for you, my king.
Preparing for you, my king.
Day and night, I prayed,
Prayed to be made love to.
My prayers have been answered.
I prayed for love.
And I received you.

Make Me Believe

Even though it may not be true,
Kiss me with passion.
Grab hold of my body and let your hands move
across my curves.
Let your lips caress mine leaving your sweet nectar
across my tongue.
Leave me breathless, and begging for air.
How a kiss can touch my soul.
Let love and a new life build there.
Removing my clothing.
Removing my mask.
Removing my pain.
Leaving me naked.
Leaving me...
Just...
Bare...
Barely able to breathe.
No longer feeling the pain.
No longer crying in the rain.
No longer running..
But.
Wanting to stay.
Wanting to receive you.
Inch by inch.
Wanting to play.
Wanting to taste.
Can you feel my hunger?
Can you scratch my itch?
As I pull you into me.

Make Me Believe

Receiving your body.
I'm inviting you to touch.
Skin that hasn't been touched,
With love.
Inviting you to kiss.
Lips that haven't been kissed,
With Passion.
Inviting you to destroy.
Walls that haven't been destroyed,
With trust.
Even though,
It may not be you.
Let's play a game of pretend.
Pretend your love for me,
Is true.

My King

I want to feel strength,
When I am with you.
I want to feel the love you have for me,
In your touch and in your kiss.
I want to know that being bonded to you, and
bounded by you,
Is a safer then walking these streets alone.
I want to know that you will move heaven and earth,
To lay next to me.
I want to know that your soul burns,
To keep me safe and warm.
I want to know that the thought of anyone jeopardizing
my safety, sets your inner beast on fire.
I want to know you plan to gently caress my body,
Massage my intelligence.
I want to know that my dreams are your dreams, and
your dreams are mine to encourage.
I want to know that it's okay to be led by you.
That you have the strength of a King.
The willingness to protect his Queen.
I want to know that for you,
Losing is not an option.
That you plan to succeed.
Reaching every goal and every dream.
I want to know that you believe every black man,
black woman, and black child deserves to be free.
So free that you will choose to educate yourself,
In order to help our dying breed.

My King

I want to know that you don't think it's all about you or
me.
It's that thought alone that has our generation
suffering greatly.
I want to know that you can be my strength when I am
weak.
On days when I just can't deal,
There's no worries because you got me.
I want to know that it's okay to believe.
In black love.
In black erotica.
In just being black like me.
I want to know that it's okay to let my Locs hang free.
That the beauty in me is all that you see.
That we have more than just sexual chemistry.
I want to know that at the end of the day
Next to me is where you crave to be.
That I am your favorite person, and your love is mine
to keep.
That you awake everyday with thoughts of me.
Thinking about marriage,
And loving me for eternity.
I want to know you have the qualities of the man that I
need.
So, that I may devote my mind, my body, and my soul
to you,
As your Queen.

Sweet Memories

On the horizon, nearsighted desires in the form of
you.
Butterfly elusiveness.
Those memories abuse my sanity.
Just out of reach.
So focused on the journey back to you.
I've lost my ability to sight-see.
Remembering moments so sweet.
So captivated by what used to be.
Wanting you so much that I've created a mirage.
Praying that if I include all this nostalgia in the mix.
My heart.
Pieces of me.
Ummmm…
Let me think.
Oh yes, photos of you and me.
All of your hopes and dreams.
That I would have created the perfect recipe to bring
you back to me.
I sleep with a pen and a pad.
Just in case,
Thoughts of you and I come together and make
movies in my dreams.
Because you and I are the screenplay to my life.
But I keep missing the lead.
I sit in the audience,
Hoping you will catch a glimpse of me.
But then it all fades away.
The smoke clears.

Sweet Memories

Reality comes and says hello.
I hate this game of peek-a-boo.
When I remove my hands from my eyes,
I see so clearly.
It's just me and not you.
Still standing on the beach,
Where I laid your ashes to rest.
The waves carried you further and further away from
me.
It's in the horizon.
You always,
Materialize for me.

Instability

There is no reason
I should be so
Out of balance.
But on the left,
And on the right,
Appears to be magnified.
Magnified by what I thought you were.
Forgive my naivety,
I don't believe there is honesty
Down the path you created.
But…
I'm…
Switching gears.
I'm…
Creating windstorms.
I'm…
Leaving dust in our past created by lust.
This…
Well-prepared road leads to my happiness.
Forgetting those passionate fights between our
superheroes.
My Kitty-women…
And your Black Knight.
No longer existing in this universe called,
My life.
This unstable land.
My decked-out pad.
It's…
Played…

Instability

Out…
Just…
A tad…
Shifting left.
Shifting right.
During this earthquake romance
I've had to move onto another fault line.
Knowing some natural disasters
Will never be forgotten.
So, as I recover,
I thank my new cross hero.
He who continues to rebuild my universe.
I say goodbye to instabilities.
I say hello to lost creativities.
There is no more naivety.
Only…
New…
Found…
Wisdom.

Just

You spark fire.
Flames filled with magic.
A hocus-pocus that blew my walls away.
As I stand breathless in my castle
I'm wondering…
How did you find my island?
See I…
Purposely tucked it away
So, it couldn't be found.
And I…
Purposely built high walls.
So, you couldn't see in.
You know I…
Purposely hid in the basement,
So, you couldn't find me.
And I'm wearing all these layers,
So, you can't touch me.
I don't want you to know how soft I am.
And…
I don't want you to know how sweet I taste.
Because then you…
Might want to dig deeper,
And get to know the real me.
I might start to drop layers.
I might start to feel.
Those things called feelings.
One day I just might wake up and believe.
That you could possibly love me.
Not everyone is trying to hurt me.

Just

I can stop using the word me,
And start believing in the word we.

When You Ask

He opened his mouth to say,
"When you gone cook for me?"
Not realizing,
She already has a mouth to feed.
Selfishly,
He only thinks about himself.
His wants and his needs.
Not a thought in his mind,
That the ingredients are not free.
If she asked,
"What you got on it?"
Or…
If she charges a fee,
Oh now, it's "she's a hoe".
or,
"How fucked up this bitch got me".
Sadly enough, he don't even see his faults.
He never stopped to calculate,
How much one meal can cost.
Let me start with something simple,
And maybe you'll start to think;
About how making you a plate can be so costly.
She pays for the lights so she can see.
The gas to cook the meat.
Her time to prepare a feast.
She pays for all the items that you wish to eat.
She covers the cost of oil.
The seasoning for the meat.

When You Ask

Still the only thing on your mind,
Is what she got to eat?
Even when she's done,
She still has to clean.
The water to wash the dishes.
The soap used to disinfect.
And all you can think about,
Is what she's cooking next.
Before you even think to say,
"When you gone feed me?"
You need to offer up enough,
To cover the cost completely.
Ultimately, you're taking her time,
Her money,
And food,
From her seed.
What woman you know
Would want to cook for
or keep
A man like that?

Validity

Respectfully, I'm admitting to submission.
My heart sings songs of love.
Lust driving my body to you nightly.
Physical attraction
Magnified by your swag.
Toy soldiers marching to a broken salute.
With your cadence as single.
Unlovely life.
Committed not.
Beneath it slowly rots.
Daggers you throw.
Piercing spirits.
Amongst your words,
Ghost from your past.
How long will you let it all control your future?
Seemingly your number one.
But not.
Oozing sex appeal.
I hook them all with my bait.
You're always so elusive.
Always getting away.
But I've captured parts of you,
And you can't understand how.
What did you call me?
I am..
THE TRUTH!

De'Vina Jackson

Therapy

How connected to him I have become,
A man who already belongs to someone.
I was drawn to him mentally.
Pulled into his world falsely.
Thinking I've finally found my king.
Allowing myself to get lost in his love.
I let go of my fears,
Allowing myself to trust him.
Not knowing he played devious games,
In order to deceive me.
He knew he couldn't be what I need.
He knew my standards he could not meet.
But instead of honesty,
He fed me lies in the form of mental treats.
So addicted to him, I couldn't believe my intuition.
Believing I could walk away as soon as my morals
came into question.
Bounded by love to a liar's game.
Unable to escape,
I rationalized my reasons to stay.
I merged it with his form of the truth, and his marriage
became okay.
Allowing him back into my bed
My home became tainted.
No longer could I be considered a respectable
woman.
I lowered my standards and accepted a man who will
never belong to me.

Therapy

No longer could I be a woman who demanded
respect.
I had lost my way.
Dumpster diving with the rest of the violated women
I was...
Just...
Like...
Them...
As I lay in my bed.
Alone cuddling with my pillows.
My broken crown by my side.
Tear-soaked sheets.
I'm realizing he will never complete me.
I will never return to being a Queen as long as I keep
hanging on to a man that does not belong to me.
For as long as he is married, he will always be
cheating with me.
I will never be a woman who behaved respectfully.
He will never belong to me.
This behavior is unbecoming of a Queen.
The Queen...
That I...
Used to be...

Your Reality

When you think they love you,
They don't.
When you think they need you,
It's not true.
When you think they want you,
Think again.
When you stop providing,
Than it's clear.
They never loved you,
My dear.
They never needed you,
Sweetheart.
They never wanted you,
Handsome.
You were just a convenience.
Providing the material things, they needed.
When you can no longer provide.
Pay attention.
The one that starts providing for you.
Was the only one that was true.

De'Vina Jackson

Unique Love

One of the simplest things seem to be the hardest to
get.
Love.
I guess it wasn't made for me just yet.
They say real women, attract real men, based on the
real-ness of their actions.
From what I can tell most men don't want real-ness in
their women's actions.
I played the games and flew the kite to attract one
that I thought was just right.
But no…
Not quite.
So here is my story.
I thought if I made myself desirable in the eyes of
men.
It would be easy for me to get
His love.
I cooked his dinner and made his plate,
Cleaned his house after working real late.
But no…
Nothing yet.
So, I prided myself on,
Watching shows,
And…
Reading books,
About…
Giving the best blows,
But no…
Nothing yet.

43

Unique Love

I heard that if I,
Lick the tip.
And…
Play with his balls.
And…
Swallow his cum,
That he will fall in love with me.
And well…
No…
Nothing yet.
Then I was told.
That if I made him,
Wait for it.
That if he had to work for it.
That if I don't sleep with him until after the third date.
That he would value me.
He will fall in love with me.
Because…
I was a woman to be respected.
But no…
Nothing yet.
So, I decided to start
Looking toward my values and morals.
I dug deep to find a him,
He who would complement me.
Financially.
Mentally.
Sexually.
Emotionally.
My equal.
But no…
Nothing yet.
And after all of that.
I was told my standards were too high.
I should settle for just simple lies.
Yeah, no…

Unique Love

Defuq?
So, I start giving out a bunch of fuck-you and
goodbyes,
To those that used to come alive between my thighs.
I delivered heavy-weight blows,
Filled with fuck-you and goodbye.
But…
Awaiting in the shadows,
Overlooked.
He watched me as I played dangerous games with
my lady parts.
And even with all of that, he still craved to make me
smile.
Even with all of that,
He still wanted to play in my garden.
Even with all of that,
He still wanted to make me happy.
Even with all of that, his goal was still to spoil me.
Still wanting to give me his
Unique love.
Doubting his true intentions, I questioned
What is love?
Besides attaching myself to some random,
As we tandem jump into the deep end.
A cesspool of cum stains, acid rains and emotional
pains.
Fighting against him and his unique love.
Wanting to believe my methods were working to keep
him at bay.
I continued to over-look him, in the shadows over
there.
Watching me.
Protecting me.
Trying to give me one of the simplest things.
His unique love.
I couldn't take it.

Unique Love

Because I needed to heal.
His unique love.
At this moment.
I'm not ready.
Not from him.
Not yet.
So, he continues to watch.
Patiently waiting.
To give me the simplest thing.
Love.
So damn hard to give, to a broken heart.
Something we all seem to forget.
But not him.
Not yet.

Vegas Weather, Vegas Life

Knowing I choose not to break,
She cries for me.
As thunder and lighting,
Dance across the sky.
Opening her soul,
She pours for me.
In the wake of this illusion.
It has caused so much pain.
It's only in my shower can I truly rain.
With help from the steam my pride remains.
Walking alone.
Somberly sweet,
Nothing…
I hear nothing.
Listening I hear,
Lies.
Only lies coming through,
I hear lies.
Coming through crystal clear,
Lies.
Filled with waves of emotions.
Rolling waves.
Silenced by your outburst.
Completing you.
You…
Separating us.
Us…
Leaves fall.
Me…

Vegas Weather, Vegas Life

Keeping us together.
You…
Like a child, you play.
You…
Kicking us apart.
This is not another sad love poem.
This is my mental strength.
Encouraged by my emotional release.
Preparing for summer.
Alone I stand.
Complete of imperfections.
Making up me.
One hundred percent of my DNA is
Made up of strong woman.

Out of The Shadows

I used to have dark nights.
Filled with slavery demons.
From the truth of "your love".
Those dark nights played tricks on my psyche,
Causing a visible reality,
To overshadow my sense of honesty.
My truth believed "your love" was a type of generosity.
The type that gave strength.
My truth believed "your love" was her salvation.
Her preventative measures from pain.
My truth grabbed ahold of "your love",
Welcomed its grace into her world.
My truth used "your love" to build a wall around her
version of the truth.
"Your love" told my version of the truth everything it
needed to hear.
My version of the truth stood proud.
Knowing it made it though your selection process.
My truth danced happy dances inside the walls of
"your love".
"Your love" would tell my version of the truth,
Stories of great warriors fighting to protect the
queendom.
My version of the truth knew "your love" would never
cause pain.
There was no reason to doubt the legends.
While a portion of my truth stood at the front gate,
Glossy-eyed and hypnotized.
What was remaining of my truth,
Nicknamed intuition,

Out of The Shadows

Slipped out the back.
Those dark forces grabbed hold of my truth's
innocence.
They began ripping my truth to shreds.
The rest of my truth could feel the pain,
But was unsure of where it was coming from.
My truth was never supposed to leave the compound.
My truth was never supposed to stop looking at the
mirage.
My truth was never supposed to be free.
My truth was never supposed to believe.
When I started, I said I used to have dark nights.
Because out of the shadows,
Came a dark knight.
That dark knight was so very different than any
warrior my truth had ever seen.
He carried weapons and armor that my psyche had
never dreamed.
He wielded potions and antidotes that knocked down
every wall in my queendom.
Before my truth could even question his motives,
He pulled out platinum and titanium,
Gold trimmings and diamond windows,
All for strength.
He reached back in his bags,
Pulled out Calla Lilies and White Roses,
Dolphins and butterflies,
All for beauty.
He then began to rebuild my truths queendom brick
by brick.
That black knight told my truth, I'm not here to kidnap
you from your queendom.
I'm just here to bring you brighter days.
He told my truth, get used to this.
Because this is what Black Knights really do.

Carnívore

Cannibalism we all partake.
Sometimes intentional.
Sometimes by mistake.
A hunger.
A thirst.
Engulfed pulling rage.
To unleash my dragon.
That beast.
Taking what I need.
I need to feed.
Cannibal.
A monster taking over me.
As they all feed on me.
Draining me of my necessities.
Depleting me.
I need to feed,
Feed on your lust.
Feed on your passion.
Daily,
I'm running tests on you.
Nightly,
I'm preparing your body for me.
Pulling away parts of your essence.
All parts inside of me.
Fulfilling my needs.
Feasting on thee.
Cannibalism.
We all need to eat.
Taking the parts of me that are incomplete,

Carnivore

I'm taking from you.
All that I need to proceed.
It's all about my need.
Focused on my greed.
Now, lay back and focus on my eyes,
As I prepare to feed.

Fairy Tales

Is this love plagued by misery?
I thought this love would rewrite my history.
Preparing me for a happy ending.
I played with his nursery rhymes.
I guess I got caught by his…
Duck…
Duck…
Goose…
I was thinking I'd have a little fun.
While I was looking for love.
I be damned.
That stupid Cupid.
And that saint they call Valentine.
They made me want to get some of his love.
And now…
I think they all sit around laughing,
At the jokes played on me.
Go ahead and roast your marshmallows.
Tell your war stories.
I spoke with my creator
He says…
Worry not my child.
Just believe.
I've created a hero.
He is on his way.
Your story has a lead.
I stay focused on the ending.
The details only build character
Right?

Fairy Tales

With every turn of the page,
We...
Draw them in.
We...
Make them want to watch.
That's when the real fun begins.
While you think I'm a damsel in distress.
Subliminally I'm saying "I love haters".
But out loud.
I'm saying...
"It's fuck all the rest".
When you're reading this story.
Remember it's my story.
And my rewrites...
The best!

News Flash

My sexual appetite is unspoken.
One I don't think you can handle.
My growth as a woman is demanding.
Proven to be too much for one man.
At night, my body aches.
For a soft and gentle touch.
A kiss.
A caress.
Full of passion and lust.
Diamonds and jewels.
They are nice.
But no, they're not enough.
I need something unexpected.
Full of stamina and robust.
My wanting and my yearning,
Is unlike any you've ever seen.
Like a volcanic awaking,
Or your most explicit dream.
Now you have no choice,
You have to release this queen.
Because the last few nights,
You just couldn't make me cream.
I know you feel defeated,
It was never my intention.
News flash love,
I've outgrown this situation.

De'Vina Jackson

Because I'm Selfish

I want to make music with you.
Beautiful symphonies of harmonic pleasure with you.
I want to practice making love with you.
Toss and turn and mess up the sheets with you.
I want to steal kisses from you.
Passionate, long and wet
Defining foreplay with you.
I want to crack jokes with you.
Play fight, you pinning me down, looking up at you.
I want to get mad at you.
Communicate, agree to disagree,
But in the end, I'm still with you.
I want to earn trust from you,
Feel lust with you,
Build and unbreakable bond, connect and grow old
with you.
I don't want to play house with you.
I want to build an empire with you.
Become your wife, creating life, raise a prince or two.
I want to create memories with you.
Celebrate holidays with you.
Have special days and anniversaries with you.
I want to plan trips with you.
Have wonderful vacations with you.
Make silly faces, pose for pictures, and toast
champagne with you.
I want to share my dreams with you.
Reach my goals with you.

Because I'm Selfish

Walk through flames, climb mountains, and be
successful with you.
I want my tears wiped by you.
When I've fallen, and can't get up, use life alert with
you.
I want to know it's true.
I want to say I love you, as you repair my broken
heart, with your 'I love you' glue.
I want to fall madly in love with you, defy gravity with
you.
Sit on a train, hold your hand on a plane, take a cruise
with you.
I want to hear a love song and think of you.
Write poems about you.
Watch a movie, read a quote, and it all remind me of
you.
I want to come home to you, cook dinner for you.
Take a shower, lay on your chest, and cuddle with
you.
I want to need to see you, but be too stubborn to tell
you.
All along knowing you need me too.
I want it all with you.
I want my day to begin and end with,
Good morning,
Good night and,
I'll always love you.

Dream-State

Just when I stop and think
I've been released.
Some simple thing snaps me back to your reality.
That I miss you,
That 'good morning, love'.
I was not enough to keep you.
Past experiences forever attaching me to you.
Memories of your sex games
Keeping you alive in my dreams.
Constantly causing my temperature to rise.
Physically feeling you as I'm imagining it.
Touching myself.
Emulating your hands.
On…
My body…
Belongs to you.
Still your slave.
Still your sex slave.
Still your submissive.
Wanting to obey.
Wanting to please.
Just when it starts to feel really good.
You disappear.
You're only in my dreams.
So, I toss and turn.
Trying to get back to you.
To the land of pretend.
The land of make believe.
Believing you want me.

Dream-State

Believing you need me.
Believing our life is unique.
It was that simple thing.
That brought me back to your reality.
And in that reality, I lived in your world.
Alive.
High on your sex game.
Alive in your presence.
High on your memories.
Just when I start to think I've been released.
A simple 'good morning, love',
Brings me back to memories of you.
Memories of us kissing like lovers do.
Like lovers destined to be.
For me it was real.
For me it was genuine.
And right now…
I really don't want to be released.
I live in my dreams.
Where we still exist.
Where it's still me.
And it's still you.
Together as us.
We are husband and wife in my dreams.

He Crossed My Mind

Quite naturally you and I.
With such strong personality.
Both full of jealousy.
Neither prepared to face reality.
Conflicted emotions.
Never minute, extremely potent.
Pleasure-filled beads of sweat.
Heated words plus feelings of neglect.
Passionate embrace.
Hunger for your touch.
Connected.
Entangled.
Maybe too much.
In such a short time,
Lust became love.
I've fallen.
Completely drowning.
But...
With you,
Hazy sightings of truth.
No need to lie,
But you do.
Complicated situations.
Aggravated conditions.
Eroding zeal.
Leaking love.
Slowly...
Drips...
To...

He Crossed My Mind

An…
End.
My inamorato.
Fading fast.
Liquid gallantry.
But still,
I yearn to be with thee.
My past.
My present.
And possibly my future.
Placed in my life for reason.
Now is it a teaching or a season?
Nevertheless…
Welcome to my world,
My love.

In Love

Every once in a while.
That feeling takes me.
My heart aches.
"In Love" breezes past my soul.
Butterflies dance in my stomach as a reminder of "In
Love" feelings.
My Idea of relationships do not exist in today's world.
Hopeless romantic, I guess.
Diving in pools of selfishness.
Confused players,
In my "In Love" life.
Games played like tambourines.
But, I don't really want to play anymore.
I want "In Love"
Falling past dreaming alone,
I want to build a home.
Falling past sleeping alone,
I want to cuddle in order to keep warm.
Falling past just sex.
I want to make love,
"In Love",
All night long.
I want "In love" pleasures.
And "In Love" commitments.
I want to make people sick with our "In Love" bliss.
I need an "In Love" friendship.
Where we communicate with just a kiss.
And every single time I think, I don't deserve this.
I'm reminded that God gave me you,

In Love

My "In Love" Gift.

Death by Winter

Standing on my frozen lake.
Frozen lake.
Frozen lake.
My frozen lake.
My beautiful treasure.
My most valued desire.
I know I can grasp it.
Before it's devoured.
My frozen lake.
It's powerful pull.
Making every single neutron in my body fire.
Rapid fire.
Rapid fire.
Making every neutron rapid fire.
The center of my frozen lake,
Seems so attainable.
Those the icy waters don't seem dangerous.
Hypothermia seems so worth it.
My potential death seems like a benefit.
Like I can profit.
Big profit.
Great profit.
My profit.
If I can just get to the middle of my frozen lake.
Blind to the plausible danger.
Deaf to the cracking ice beneath my feet.
Incapable of deciphering the warning signs.
Ignorant to the amount if pain it brings.
My frozen lake.

Death by Winter

Frozen lake.
My greatest desire is in the center.
Of my frozen lake.
And though I know I should
Walk slowly.
And though I know I should
Move with caution.
I crave the center of my frozen lake.
Ice crumbling beneath me.
I realized...
The center of my frozen lake,
Is a mere fairy tale.
Last step.
Last breath.
My frozen gives away.
My frozen lake breaks.
My frozen lake deceives.
When I felt safe,
My frozen lake was always going to break.
Frozen lake.
Frozen lake.
My final death was,
Midway to the epicenter of my...
Frozen lake.

She is The Other Me

Whiskey-coated whispers touched my ears.
With him, she awakes.
Her carnal cravings reveal themselves in my eyes.
She is always in need of release.
She craves many positions.
She craves many lovers.
But most of all.
Tonight.
She craves him.
She imagined being fucked inside the White House.
On top of those presidential sheets.
She imagined taking her lover.
In the park.
On the beach.
In the bathroom at a five-star hotel.
She wanted him to taste her.
While people push baskets around them in the frozen
food section.
She was bold,
Where I was not.
She wanted him in my mouth.
She wanted him deep down my throat.
She wanted us to try anal.
She was strong when I was weak.
She wanted him to give us pain.
She wanted him to give us pleasure.

She is The Other Me

She wanted him.
And…
She wanted me to want him.
When I was unsure.
She had no doubts.
She wanted me to walk up to him.
Take his hand,
Place it between my legs and tell him.
Touch this.
Tease this.
Caress this.
She wanted me to look into his eyes and dominate
him.
But, I couldn't do it.
Once again, she has had enough of me.
She took over me.
For him, she commanded me.
She controlled me.
And I became.
A jagabat.
A wabean.
I became a woman of questionable morals.
I became one who lives the wild life.
For him, I became a nocturnal female.
I became a whore on the prowl for him.
She took over me.
She and I became we.
I became bold.
Fearless.
I became a sexual goddess.
I became confident.
I walked up to him in slow motion.
I caressed his crotch.
I made his manhood rise.
I couldn't care less who began to watch.
I became her.

She is The Other Me

She took over me.
I was Capri.

De'Vina Jackson

Random Acts

It started with a conversation and ended with
You know…
Because I was so very blunt.
Hey, I want to fuck you.
No time for simple pleasantries.
No fake, "How do you do's?"
Just a simple random act.
Just me on top of you.
I didn't want to know his name.
I didn't have time for his "Playa Playa" games.
I just wanted to cum,
All over his face.
I slipped him my number with a simple phrase.
Just let me know whats up,
But we're not using my place.
I know what I want.
It includes,
Legs shaking,
And
Headboard banging.
I just need to know if you can, well…
Make me cum all over the place.
That's right you heard me.
I guess as a woman,
I'm not allowed to talk this way.
I'm supposed to just be used.
Ummm right.
Yeah, no.
I'm keeping it real.

Random Acts

I'm going to use you.
I don't plan on falling in love.
I don't plan on making it work.
I just plan on well, you know…
Cumin' until it hurts.
Pardon my bluntness.
Pardon my speech.
I don't want you to be confused,
This is all about me.
Don't care what tales you tell.
Don't care what lies you speak.
As long as you know the truth.
This was just a random act,
This was just me fucking you.

Who Really Knows?

It's only when I'm truly alone do I realize everything
that's missed.
No kisses to my lips.
No fingers in my hair.
No one to wipe a shedding tear.
When thoughts run wild in my mind,
Disturbing my sleep and effecting my grind.
It's only then I really realize how alone I am.
With no one to listen.
And no one to fight.
No one to care if I'm wrong or I'm right.
When my walls seem to fall,
And it all seems too much.
There's never anyone with strength to be my crutch.
It's only then I really realize how alone I am.
When the weight seems too heavy,
My heart is filled with worry,
There's no one there to help in a hurry.
No bitter sweet memories,
No one for me to marry.
No "I love you"'s, no "I do"'s
No "it's me for you".
All I hear is silence speaking,
Telling me how alone I am.
No champagne to share.
No chance of cuddles here.
No inside jokes,
No cute loving pokes.
No King for a Queen,

Who Really Knows?

No one to put me to sleep.
All alone in this Cali King.
Just pillows, sheets, and me.
With every chill I feel.
I know the loneliness is real.
In that moment, I realize,
How alone I really feel.
On this sleepless night,
I'll read and I'll write.
About how alone I am,
In my bed late at night.

Sight-Seeing

An Intimate journey into pleasure-filled pain.
Take a ride with me to ecstasy.
Where lust,
Passion,
And eroticism,
Are the rules of my game.
The only material needed to play is your body.
My canvas.
My perfect Santa sleigh.
Riding all day.
Bring joy to my world.
I'm given you permission,
To enter the most fruitful field.
Relish in her beauty.
Fall in love with her skill.
In the mist of all the chaos.
Entering her cave gives you the greatest thrill.
Gives you peace of mind.
You know…
Those chills down your spine.
You know…
The kind of pleasure that starts at your toes.
And your body tenses up.
Paralysis sets in.
I take over all movement.
Giving you more than just a hand.
Bringing your orgasm to the head.
Teasing you to the point of torture.
That pleasure.

Sight-Seeing

Filled.
Pain.
Take a journey with me.
Once we arrive.
Prepare for serenity.
No need to practice.
Your body,
I read.
When your muscles tighten up.
I know I'm doing a good deed.
Last but not least.
Your number one, I must be.
If you're ready,
Your personal paradise awaits.
As your guide,
Preparing to fulfill all your needs.
I say to you.
Relax, baby.
Enjoy your treats.
Once you realize they will never be me.
This type of indulgence is yours to keep.
Don't wait too long to pick a seat.
No tour waits forever.
Eventually,
We all must leave.

Intoxication

It was in that moment,
I knew he was a drug I could no longer resist.
My addiction to him became intense.
I welcomed the high.
Its euphoric bliss.
Moments ago, I overdosed on a kiss.
A kiss I normally wouldn't have indulged in.
Because of our past,
And the lack of physical contact.
It made me crave his lips.
Fingers through hair.
Nails on back.
Me in his lap.
His rise and my fall.
Complimenting my pace.
His push and my pull,
During this orgasmic race.
His lips at my ear.
My lips at his neck.
His hips rising creating an arch in my back.
In a bed, we don't normally share.
That separates us at night.
I gave myself to him.
In our familiar way.
Giving into the passion that,
Only we can create.
Love not lust.
Mixed with hurt.
Hidden under pain.
Pain not lost,
But…

Intoxication

Hidden under lust.
For on this one night.
We gave way to the hurt.
And dined in the memory of our love.
Not concerned with our past arguments.
Just riding the waves of pure adult bliss.
Wondering if one day,
We will again grow as one.

I Am Simple

I am simple,
So not unique.
Not the perfect person,
Of which you speak.
In this time of struggle,
Yes, I stand upright.
Not because I'm ready for the fight.
It's because I'm looking over the crowd.
Wondering if I need to be light on my feet.
Planning a line of escape somehow.
Partly because of my recluse-like nature.
Deep within these protective walls.
No need to seek cover.
No stranger danger.
I ask to you.
What is it that you seek within me?
How could I have touched you so deeply?
My damaged soul.
How can you trust me completely?
Are you sure you know the real me?
Because I don't.
That ferocious stare.
Gazing contently.
I'm strong.
I'm tough.
I can be rough.
I hope you know,
You can say what you want.
It won't hurt me.

I Am Simple

Be honest and upfront.
Causing no pain here.
I've been through a lot.
No rivers cried.
No worries.
No boats afloat.
All not to be found.
Worry not of my safety,
Care not of my feelings.
Dwell on your pain, and anguish.
Right now, my world is flat.
Ending where the sky touches the sea.
Maybe one day I'll have a full circle,
Maybe one day I'll believe.
You know.
Unity.
But for now.
I am simple,
Not even close to unique.
I can't be that perfect one that you seek.

Cause and Effect

It's not you who inspires me,
It's the things you do that inspire me.
Your actions cause a reaction,
Within my body's chemistry.
Fireworks explode rapidly.
When you enter me,
Enter you,
Into my mind.
Here comes your philosophy.
Breathing deeply.
With these shallow breaths.
I can't catch my breath.
I'm communicating,
With your soul.
As you soul search.
I found it.
See baby.
Catering to your needs,
Is what I've been created for.
Nope.
Not less of a woman,
I am every woman,
What every woman should desire,
And aspire to be.
One who tames lions easily.
I've been given the key.
With this key and opportunity,
To help you become free.
Free from stereotypes.

Cause and Effect

Free from loneliness.
Free from nothingness.
Free to be with me.
What you need to understand,
Is behind every lonely man,
Is his shadow.
Not a strong woman rubbing his back.
Nor giving him strength.
Nor providing nourishment.
With them you will always be lonely.
She's not like me for a reason,
She can never be a Queen.
You won't get empowerment.
She doesn't know how to endear.
Meant to be,
We...
Wait...
I'm starting to think we are not.
How easily I turned away,
When you pushed today.
I guess I no longer have it in me.
You.
That is,
Your love.
Like I said.
You no longer inspire me.
It's the things you've done,
That inspired me to leave.

Exclusive

Well,
Exclusively me.
To the point where I don't want to share you.
And you are committed to,
Not sharing me.
You focus on,
Completing me.
Exclusive epitome.
Where you agree,
To only be with me.
You see our solidarity.
Makes them compare me,
To everyone in your past you see.
Exclusive, I want you to be.
Parts of me are shielded.
Guarded.
Protected.
And hidden.
It's here in secrecy.
I yearn for that exclusivity.
I know I make you believe,
That I don't care if it's you for me.
I'm dying for that exclusivity.
That only you can give to me.
I want you to cater to me,
Only because you love to please.
I need someone exclusive to me.
Someone who is fit for a queen.
Dying to be inside of me.

Exclusive

Resting peacefully beside me,
Wanting,
Craving,
Needing me.
See all I want is exclusivity.
Someone who is happy to see,
The perfect imperfection.
Which is me.

Awareness

In the wake of my own personal storm,
I find comfort in your touch.
Far from the physical,
Your mental hold shelters me.
Your ability to catch my falling tears from miles away,
Not only soothes me but excites my alter ego.
I…
Needing to be held.
Her…
Needing to be stroked.
Together…
Both needing you in our own individual way.
We both welcome your presence.
Relax within our arms.
Vacation within our valleys.
Scuba dive in our oceans.
Leaving us both breathless.
As she craves your physical.
I crave your mental.
Needing to be reached by the depths of your core.
So that we may converse, in the most natural way.
Our way.
With words and secrets and limbs and kisses.
Our interaction makes me forget all the reasons why it
won't work.
Our interactions make me believe in all the reasons
why it will work.
Our interactions leaves flashbacks on my
subconscious like waves crashing on the shore.

Awareness

Our interactions swaddle my mind.
Holding me close and snug.
It could be a text.
A phone call.
Kisses on the lips.
Just the thought of you relaxes my soul.
Also prepares my hips.
Not at all feeling betrayed by my body.
I welcome it.
Not at all trying to resist future bliss.
Completely giving into it.
And as I lay here all alone,
With thoughts of you floating through my head
sensually like a butterfly kiss.
With ache and hunger for your dick.
My soul relaxes and my body wets its lips.
As I play in my heaven,
With memories of your mental and physical kiss.

It's What You Need

I kind of like it when you get all in your feelings.
When you get all upset about our personal dealings.
Right now the only reason you're so flexed.
Is because you need some of my angry sex.
No sweet soft kisses.
No passionate caress.
Just skin slapping skin.
Pulling hair.
Making a mess.
I know that you already crave me.
You're trying hard to avoid an addiction to me.
Just let it go.
Don't fight it.
It will all happen naturally.
And we can get back to those things that make you
happy.
Raise your voice.
Get mad.
Yell, if need be.
I know you need angry sex.
You need to be inside me.
Spank me.
Bite me.
Pull my hair.
Release those frustrations,
Then bury yourself in there.
Pull off my pants.
Rip my panties.
Do whatever you need to get to my juice box.

It's What You Need

You can take it all off,
Just don't remove my socks.
And today...
Right now...
Your face is so perplexed.
Clam down I know.
You just need angry sex.
It could have been.
Something I said.
That made you so
Upset with me.
So just turn me around
Grab my hips,
And fuck me as hard as can be.
While you're back there.
Smack my ass.
Leave hand prints if you must.
Make sure.
You.
Fuck the anger.
Out of you.
With...
Every...
Single...
Thrust...
I actually like
When you get mad at me
It's such a fucking rush.
So, you can.
Fuck me.
Like you.
Hate me.
Fuck me until you bust.
Doggy style.
On top of me.
Or fuck me sideways.

It's What You Need

It's whatever you need,
To get this pussy the right way.
While you stroke it real deep.
I'll be moaning real loud.
But you need angry sex.
So, you can take your,
Ass to sleep.

De'Vina Jackson

Why Karma Why?

Somedays I wonder if karma is playing games with
my script.
Which lifetime did I play so violently with my toys and
earn this role?
The black flame that has engulfed my heart,
Making it impossible to claim.
Must be a result of losing karma's game.
When peace at night is so elusive that sleep is a
luxury.
It's time to beg for karma's release.
Begging for karma's release is never easy.
Who blows smoke away from a karma controlled
heart?
Who rebuilds a karma-damaged vessel?
Why did karma come out and direct my movie?
Aimlessly I navigate through tadpole pools.
Drowning due to karma's weight.
How can I find karma's ladders?
When all I seem to stumble across is karma's chutes.
Losing at karma's vile game of foot in caboose.
Seems like I'm getting my dose of karma times dos.
Or times deux…
I mean two.
I don't recall earning karma's rough play.
I mean usually I like it rough, but not from karma.
No way.
No definitely not from karma.
Why has karma claimed this sleepless beauty?

Why Karma Why?

Why has karma deemed this life beauty's
punishment?
Usually, I don't live in moments of regret.
But when my moments involve karma's
transgression,
How can I not be full of regret?
How did karma find me here?
In this life.
Did I leave a trail of bread crumbs for karma to
follow?
Did someone give karma directions to my lifeless life?
Ummm karma…
Really?
Why?
Cuz honestly?
I'm just asking.
Haven't I played your game enough?
Haven't I suffered enough?
Haven't I cried enough?
Karma, why do you continue to follow me in this life?
Please tell me what I did?
What did I do wrong to upset you?
Which life did I…
Damn, I just bit my tongue and broke a nail.
(Sigh)
So, I'm going to huddle in this corner.
Hiding from karma's sight.
Close my eyes and pray.
Dear Lord please,
Save me from karma's bite.

When I Wasn't Looking

One nice relaxing morning.
Full of peaceful sleep and warm embrace.
The sweetest dreams.
And then I woke up.
As one single.
Solitary.
Tear.
Trickled down my face.
Until we meet again,
In this time and this space.
Memories created will float around my head like
butterfly kisses.
Serenity.
Tranquility.
Along With,
Sensuality.
Intoxicating me.
My drug of choice is you.
So high that I hover over the heavens.
In our game of capture the flag.
You've found a way to capture my heart.
Chiseled away the stone.
The hate.
And all of the hurt.
Ability to see the possibility of 24hrs of happiness.
But you…
So deep into your life without me.
So unfazed by what is developing.
My question to you is,

When I Wasn't Looking

How does it feel?
No.
Nasty.
Not that.
Not kitty.
How does it feel to know that I love you?
How does it feel to know that you have me?
How does it feel to know that I say
I belong to you?
And we aren't even a couple.
You are.
The epitome of bliss.
As you capitalize on my body.
Opening flood gates.
Discovering new territories.
Exploring new lands.
Opening all parts of,
My mind.
My body.
My soul.
Full speed ahead.
I seem to proceed,
Leaping past Lust,
Passionate Love making,
Or so I'd like to think.
This sexual awakening,
Is only a one-sided pull.
Drowning me in the salvation.
That salvation, is your tender touch.
Completely stunned by your style.
Everything about you motivates me to try new things.
To break my own rules.
To take off my blinders.
To remove some…
Restrictions.
To remove some clothing.

When I Wasn't Looking

One nice relaxing morning,
Full of peaceful sleep and warm embrace.
In that sweetest dreams.
I realized I was in love.

De'Vina Jackson

November, 2014

How can I be expected to be thankful
When my holidays are filled with bloodshed?
When I should be gathering with family over the
dinner table.
Instead,
I'm gathering with family over a hospital bed.
Asking prayer warriors to save his legs, when one
piece of my heart is already dead.
Being thankful is the furthest thing from my mind.
When a mother loses her son over objects that shine.
And one could lose use of his legs because he went
for a ride.
Trying to be her strength,
As she lays her son to rest.
Only to be shattered once again by the news of
paralyzed legs.
When one bad decision cost a son his life,
Another bad decision almost cost another his life.
Again, I ask how can I be thankful when the holidays
are filled with bloodshed?
I wonder if I was a bigger presence could I have
saved two.
The son with his huge smile would have given you his
shoes.
I'm supposed to forgive when things are at their worst.
I'm supposed to remember to trust in his word.
A mother should never beat her son into the earth.
Especially with only an 18 year head-start from the
time of his birth.

November, 2014

My holiday seeps crimson painfully attached to my
soul.
So how can I be thankful when their hands I cannot
hold.
Restless nights.
Their faces out of sight.
Trying to keep calm when my emotions are not right.
And I'm supposed to be thankful?
But it's impossible when my holidays are filled with so
much bloodshed.

Why?

I can't give this much of me,
To a shell of a man.
Going through, the motions of life.
Up.
Down.
And All Around.
Your emotions fall with no attachments.
Noncommittal pleasures are fun.
Right?
It's only temporary.
Right?
Selfishly you give words of endearment,
Made to keep, not to protect.
Claims of personal hurt spilling over lying eyes.
I've listened to that song of yours,
A bittersweet goodbye.
Your tearless cries.
Playing games with my wet eyes.
Bittersweet aggressive sighs pleasures this immortal
guy.
But you shell of a man.
Are an imperial imposter.
With failing communications skills,
We fall distantly out of love.
My fight to be understood,
Shouldn't be a fight to be heard.
Cloudy memories of amazing love making.
One-sided pleasures.
Painful pleasures.

Why?

Ignored equally.
Aggressive dominance.
Nope. I'm done.
I am uniquely that criminal you can't capture.
World renowned like,
Where in the world is…
You better get a few more stamps on your passport,
You street smart-hero.
And stop playing games with this world-wrecking
traveler.
You can't navigate the nautical miles.
Queens are some men's life-long dream.
Way beyond the realm of "a shell of a man's" mind.
You can claim you want to be.
The equivalent of a queen's dream.
However, you can't even be the king in your own
dreams.
So imperial imposter.
Keep using quotes and subliminals to get attention.
Because your actions speak for a shell of a man.
Not the king you claim to be.

De'Vina Jackson

About the Author

De'Vina Jackson was born and raised in San Francisco, California. De'Vina spent most of her childhood in San Francisco before her parents moved to Antioch, California in 1996. In 2005, she moved to Las Vegas, Nevada, where she currently resides. As a single mother of an eight year old boy she is inspired by the lost days of respect, honor and falling in love with your soul-mate. Ms Jackson is currently a bartender in one of the oldest gentlemen's clubs in the great city of Las Vegas. De'Vina can be contacted by email at DevinaThePoet@gmail.com, and she will respond personally to all emails.